INTRODUCTION

**Welcome to
The Natural History
Museum.
We hope that this
book will encourage
you to discover all
the Museum has to
offer and serve as an
interesting souvenir
of your visit.**

Divided into Life and Earth Galleries,
The Natural History Museum offers a
full range of lively, innovative
exhibitions about the natural world. In
addition to the exhibitions you will
discover a programme of special
events, including films, workshops,
lectures and guided tours.
But the Museum is not only a dynamic
exhibition centre - it is also a major
scientific research institution. Behind
the scenes more than 300 scientists
study the diversity of nature using the
Museum's vast and unrivalled
collections. Some of their work is
highlighted in this guide.
We hope that you enjoy your visit and
will come again soon.

Neil Chalmers
Director
The Natural History Museum, London

HIGHLIGHTS

Left: Diplodocus skeleton
Central hall
Circle: Insect in Amber.
From collection in
**Palaeontology
department.**

Top: Earthquake experie
Story of the Earth
Centre: Giant quadrasco
Ecology
Bottom: Sir Hans Sloane
carved *Nautilus* shell.
**Minerals rocks and
meteorites**

Revealing research

What you won't see on display are the hundreds of scientists working on research projects involving plants, animals, minerals and fossils. Yet their work is a vital part of world science, and can affect your daily life. Throughout this guide, we've highlighted some of the Museum's research projects in boxes coloured like this one.

The Museum is an important natural history publisher. We produce academic texts for specialists, guides for amateur naturalists, books to accompany our exhibitions, and a range of interesting and well-produced titles for readers of all ages.

We've highlighted a few in this guide on red 'book spines' like these...

Top left: Lifesize model of a blue whale.
Discovering mammals
Centre left: Detail of terra cotta carvings.
Life galleries
Bottom left: Giant foetus.
Human biology

Top: Ants cutting leaves.
'Creepy-crawlies'
Bottom: Interactive video about memory.
Human biology

Centre right: Number 1 Crawley House.
'Creepy-crawlies'

DINOSAURS

In *Dinosaurs* new scientific evidence and state-of-the-art design have combined to give an updated and comprehensive view of dinosaur life.

Models, illustrations, animation and interactive video techniques, and, of course, fossil specimens are used in this extensive exhibition, helping to piece together our knowledge from clues left behind between 230 and 65 million years ago.

High above the gallery, a 70 metre raised walkway provides one of London's most dramatic experiences as 14 large dinosaur skeletons can be seen, sensationally suspended in mid-air. The spectacle of three roaring, life-size robotic carnivores feeding on a large herbivore, still in its death throes, leads on to displays showing the lifestyle of these impressive creatures that excite the imagination of adults and children the world over.

Dinosaurs lived on Earth for about 160 million years, but they became extinct, fairly abruptly, about 60 million years before the first humans appeared. In the exhibition you can see the fossilized remains of many different kinds of dinosaur ranging from the huge to the comparatively small.

Above: Too realistic for comfort, three *Deinonychus* feast on a freshly killed *Tenontosaurus*
Circle: Triceratops skeleton

Right: Mounted skeleton - *Dromaeosaurus*
Far right: Structure of *Albertosaurus'* leg - model

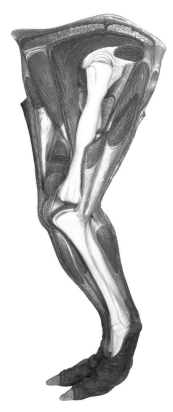

hey have been found in rocks from many parts of the world, including ritain, and recent expeditions are still iscovering astonishing new species. here must be many more for us to nd yet. The only direct evidence we ave of what dinosaurs were like comes om the fossils we are lucky enough to nd. The hard parts of the body, the ones and teeth are the most usual ossils to find, but we occasionally ome across other remains such as eggs r impressions of skin. Skeletons are nly rarely found complete and it is ifficult to piece together the fragments o reconstruct a whole animal.

n order to work out what dinosaurs vere like in life we need to use the nowledge we already have about oday's animals. By understanding how he skeletons of modern creatures reflect heir way of life, we can begin to piece ogether the clues the dinosaurs left ehind them.

Dinosaurs were reptiles but they varied normously in size, shape and lifestyle. Nevertheless, they all had some haracteristics in common: they all lived n land, could not fly and walked on traight legs which were tucked underneath their bodies. Some of the best known dinosaurs like *Tyrannosaurus* vere aggressive meat eaters, but many nore were placid vegetarians that prowsed the countryside in herds. Some of these were fleet of foot and could print away from attackers, others such as *Triceratops* were massively protected by an array of horns and spikes while *Euoplocephalus* was armour plated and wielded a vicious tail club.

There is still a good deal of argument about why dinosaurs became extinct so suddenly about 65 million years ago. Some most imaginative theories have been suggested. One of the most believable suggests that the world's climate changed suddenly - perhaps as a result of a massive meteorite striking the Earth - and that the dinosaurs were not able to adapt quickly enough to the new conditions. But there are other plausible ideas as well and the debate continues. The dinosaurs, however, do not, having been supplanted in importance by mammals. They leave as their closest descendants the birds, which very likely evolved from small meat-eating dinosaurs.

'Claws' - the Surrey dinosaur

In 1983 William Walker, an amateur fossil hunter, came across an enormous claw bone in a Surrey clay pit. A team of palaeontologists from The Natural History Museum excavated the site and uncovered many more bones that they identified as the remains of a previously unknown dinosaur that lived 124 million years ago. Scientists named the new dinosaur *Baryonyx walkeri*, although it became better known by its nickname 'Claws'.

In the Museum's palaeontology laboratory, scientists carefully separated the bones from the surrounding rock, and then pieced together a large part of the skeleton. By working out the size and position of the muscles, they concluded that 'Claws' walked mostly on its back legs and that it ate flesh including fishes. The great claw may have been used for hooking these out of lakes, rivers and marshes that existed in southern England during the early Cretaceous period.

Above left: Full size head - *Tyrannosaurus rex*
Left: Reconstruction of a *Maiasaura* nest

The *Dinosaurs* exhibition was sponsored by the following:

The Ronson Foundation,
Laura and Barry Townsley,
Angela and Harvey Soning,
John Duggan
  (Cabra Estates plc),
Garry H. Weston
  (Associated British Foods plc),
The Esmée Fairbairn
  Charitable Trust,
David Davies & John Bryant
  (Margram plc),
Nazmu Virani
  (Control Securities plc),
Lex Service plc.

The Natural History Museum
Book of Dinosaurs by Tim Gardom
with Angela Milner (scientific adviser)

ECOLOGY

The *Ecology* exhibition looks at how living things interact with one another and with their environment to form thriving communities. The exhibition is sponsored by British Petroleum.

Near the entrance to the exhibition you will see a series of large spheres representing air, earth, water and the Sun's energy, the essential ingredients of life.

A display representing the Serengeti Plain in the dry season follows. Ecology is the study of connections: how do the Serengeti creatures survive the long dry period? What links acacia trees, impala and vultures? Ecology fits these different pieces of information together to build up a whole picture.

Water is one vital link. Without it life could not exist. A vast video wall enables you to follow the water cycle... vapour rises up from the oceans, clouds form, rain tumbles to the land below, plants and animals take in the life-giving liquid, and rivers carry it back downstream, bearing nutrients to the ocean. Few people realize how important trees are to climate, recycling massive amounts of water back into the atmosphere.

Because essentials such as sunlight and water are available in different amounts across the globe, communities take different shapes. In the oceans, light and nutrients decide how a community forms, whereas on land the kind of plant and animal life depends on the climate, as you'll see in our Stonehenge-like display.

Above: Seen here from above, the giant video wall follows the water cycle
Circle: The struggle for energy - the carnivorous Bengal Tiger feeding on a Blackbuck

Top: Step into the leaf factory
Bottom: The *Ecology* gallery

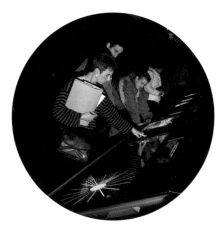

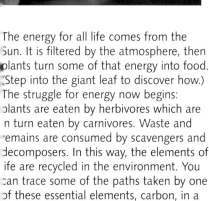

The energy for all life comes from the Sun. It is filtered by the atmosphere, then plants turn some of that energy into food. (Step into the giant leaf to discover how.) The struggle for energy now begins: plants are eaten by herbivores which are in turn eaten by carnivores. Waste and remains are consumed by scavengers and decomposers. In this way, the elements of life are recycled in the environment. You can trace some of the paths taken by one of these essential elements, carbon, in a computer game.

Ecology also looks at how communities change... and the most dramatic changes of all are being caused by human beings. Our species is bulldozing its way across the planet, destroying organisms whose value we do not even know. Is there a way for us to live in the world without destroying it? Can we preserve Earth's greatest treasure - its wealth of natural variety? It is the responsibility of each and every one of us to do so.

Top: Learning about the source of energy for all life - the sun
Centre: Experience the sights and sounds of a rainforest
Bottom: Examining marine ecosystems

Above: "In our hands rests the future of natural diversity and the essential connections that allow life to flourish here on earth" - the 'Green Man'

Global Ecology by Colin Tudge

Nature at Work: Introducing Ecology

What is a Rain Forest? by P Whitfield

Plants for People by Anna Lewington

DISCOVERING

Suspended from the gallery ceiling for over 50 years, the life-size model of a blue whale now forms a dramatic centrepiece to this modern exhibition which invites you to explore the world of mammals.

The exhibition has two sections, one on the ground floor and the other on the balcony. The ground floor exhibits give you an opportunity to view modern mammals alongside their fossil ancestors, and to learn about mammalian evolution.

A good starting point is *Arsinoitherium*, a strange, extinct mammal which lived 35 million years ago and is thought to be related to all the other mammals in the exhibition.

Present-day African and Asian elephants are one group whose evolution can be traced back through many stages. One of their most primitive ancestors was a small swamp-dwelling animal called *Moeritherium*.

The largest group of hoofed mammals is the artiodactyls. All have an even number of toes on each foot. Hippopotamuses, camels, deer and goats are just a few of those featured in the gallery.

Below: Both whales and rhinos are mammals in danger of extinction

Circle: The remains of *Arsinoitherium* were found in Egypt near the ancient tomb of Queen Arsinoe

MAMMALS

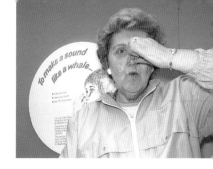

Above: Hold your nose, close your mouth and say 'oh' three times!

Left: The structure of their skeletons suggests that whales may have evolved from land-living animals
Centre: The cavernous mouth of a hippo
Bottom: African and Indian elephants

Above: Horses' and elephants' legs *are* different!
Below: Cetaceans, even when young, are superbly adapted to life in water

Stranded

To find out more about the biology of cetaceans, the Museum registers details of all the whales, dolphins and porpoises that are reported stranded on Britain's shores. On average, about 50 strandings are recorded each year by coastguards, who fill in an identification form supplied by the Museum. The completed form is then used by the scientists to identify what species the stranded cetacean is and add it to the records.
Between 1967 and 1986 there were 946 strandings involving 1117 animals - mostly common porpoises, pilot whales and common dolphins. The largest animal that has ever lived - the blue whale - has also been recorded, but not since the 1920s.

rtiodactyls are adapted to a wide
nge of habitats. Those living in the
rctic tundra, musk oxen for example,
ust keep warm, so they have thick fur
oats. Camels survive the heat of the
esert by possessing a remarkable
stem that allows their body
mperature to drop during the cool
esert night so they begin each day with
lower than normal body temperature.
live mainly in water, hippos have
nall eyes set high on the skull and
ostrils that can be closed. They can
old their breath for as long as four
inutes!
n the balcony you will be able to
scover more about the mammals
hich spend all their lives in water.
ost of this area is devoted to
etaceans, which include whales,
orpoises and dolphins.

Here you can listen to songs of different whales, follow their migrations and uncover some of the possible reasons why whales lose their way and become stranded.
Dolphins hunt for their food by sending out clicking sounds and picking up the echoes. A computer exhibit shows how they do this. Other displays contain information about how these fascinating animals breed and the importance of their colours.
Also on the balcony is a video of sirenians, or sea cows. Their strange shape led many early sailors to mistake them for mermaids.
You can discover some of the other extraordinary mammals on the mammal balcony, on the first floor of the Central Hall.

The Natural History of the Primates
by J R & P H Napier

Horse Power
by J Clutton-Brock

A Natural History of Domesticated Mammals
by J Clutton-Brock

Below: Discover how different areas of the brain cortex control our actions

Inside the outer layer of your brain
E4

of the cortex are responsible for different things:

This exhibition is about you. It has sections that tell you about the growth and development of your body and mind, and others where you are invited to think about the way you do things.

Our bodies are made up of millions of tiny units called cells but each of us began life as just a single cell - a fertilized ovum. A special slide programme traces the growth of a human embryo in the mother's womb, from this one cell to a fully-formed baby.

Fighting a deadly disease

Schistosomiasis is a disease which affects around 200 million people in 74 tropical and sub-tropical countries. It is caused by microscopic worms called schistosomes whose larvae develop in certain aquatic snails. After leaving the snails, larvae penetrate the skin of humans and animals exposed to contaminated water. The bladder and liver may be affected, resulting in the severely debilitating disease - bilharzia.
Different kinds of both schistosomes and snails are often extremely difficult to tell apart. Museum scientists use biochemical and molecular biological techniques to identify the different species and thus provide vital information for the control of the disease.

Circle: Information from the outside world reaches our brains through the senses

BIOLOGY

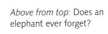

ou have ever wondered how you
ve, you will have the opportunity to
dy the bones in your skeleton, as well
he muscles that make bones move.
will also discover that it is nerves
t make muscles pull.

st of the nerve cells in your body are
centrated in your brain and spinal
d. Your brain controls almost all your
ons and many of the things you do
in response to information gathered
our sense organs and nervous
em. As well as gathering information
n outside the body, your brain also
eives messages from within it. It
ures that wherever you are and
atever you are doing, conditions
de your body, such as temperature,
gen and water content, stay more or
the same.

dy processes are not only controlled
nerves. Hormones, chemical
ssengers carried in your blood, are
important. You can find out where
our body these substances are
duced and something about the
cesses that they control, including
wth, digestion and puberty.

through our lives we learn about the
rld and store the experiences we
e as memories. Exhibits show you
t learning takes place all the time
d changes the way we do things.
m the moment we are born we begin
explore. By constant interaction with
surroundings we discover more
ut the things around us.

we grow older we develop new
ntal abilities that allow us to solve
blems we have never encountered
ore, using reason and logic. By doing
our understanding of the world
ntinues to grow...

Above: Model of an
unborn baby, seven
months after fertilization

Above from top: Does an
elephant ever forget?

A lesson in language from
extraterrestrials!

Muscle power moves
bones

Find out where your
glands are and which
hormones they produce

The Human Machine
by R McNeil Alexander FRS

Why Does My Heart Beat?
by P Whitfield & R Whitfield

Human biology: an exhibition of ourselves

There are some 20 000 species of fishes - more than all other vertebrate animals put together. A few fishes, such as sharks and rays, have skeletons made out of cartilage, but most of the world's familiar species have bony skeletons.

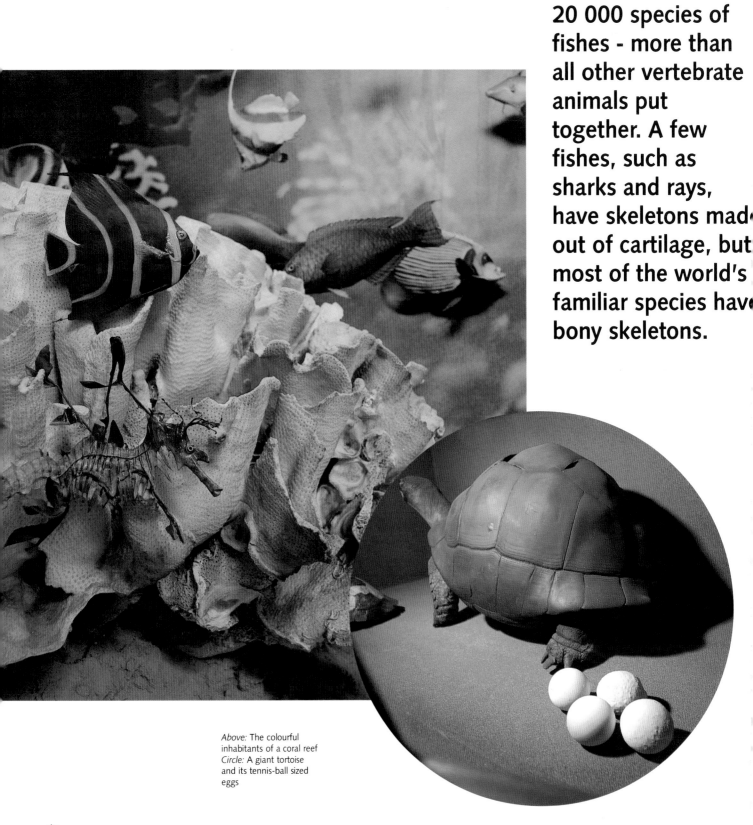

Above: The colourful inhabitants of a coral reef
Circle: A giant tortoise and its tennis-ball sized eggs

AMPHIBIANS & REPTILES

A soldier fish on guard

...display of the bony fishes ...ows the great variety within ...is group. You can also ...amine some unusual types, ...ch as the flying fishes, the ...minous and venomous ...ecies as well as the more ...miliar British marine and ...eshwater species.

...addition, there is an opportunity to ... a coelacanth. Previously known only ...m fossils, coelacanths were thought to ...ve been extinct for over 70 million ...rs. But, in 1938, a trawler working ... the coast of South Africa caught a ... which was later identified as a ...lacanth - a living fossil! Since then ...r 100 specimens have been caught ... the Comoro Islands, north of ...dagascar and they have been filmed ...derwater.

...phibians were the first vertebrate ...mals to live part of their lives on land, ...t their skin loses moisture easily and ...ir eggs have no watertight shell. ...nsequently, all amphibians need ...ess to water to breed.

...st people recognize frogs and toads ...amphibians but newts, salamanders ...d worm-like caecilians are also ...luded in this group. In fact, there are ...re than 4000 species of amphibians, ...st of which live in warm or tropical ...as.

...ptiles do not depend on water for ...eding because their eggs have a ...gh waterproof covering. With their ...atively watertight skin, many reptiles, ...h as lizards and snakes, are able to ... in areas where there is very little ...ter.

Reptiles also include crocodiles, tortoises, terrapins, turtles and strange lizard-like animals from New Zealand called tuataras. Throughout the world, there are more than 6000 species of reptiles but only six are found in the British Isles.

Carpet killer

'Flying death of Rajputana' is one of the vivid names given to the brightly coloured and highly venomous carpet viper found in India and across central Africa. Carpet vipers cause more serious bites to humans than any other group of snakes, and consequently have attracted considerable medical attention.

Treatment, however, is not straightforward - anti-venom prepared in one place is often ineffective when used elsewhere. This fact led scientists to suspect that carpet vipers from different regions, although virtually indistinguishable, produced different venom and might belong to separate species. By carefully comparing the anatomies of African and Asian carpet vipers, Museum scientists have now confirmed the species difference. It is hoped that this anatomical approach, combined with chemical studies of carpet viper venoms will lead to the development of more effective anti-venoms.

Far left: It is safe to smile at this crocodile!
Left: White striped poison frogs from South America

Above: Life-size termite
mound rises high into
the gallery
Circle: Dare you enter
1 Crawley House?

This exhibition focuses on arthropods, the animal group that includes centipedes, crabs, spiders and insects.

Eight out of ten living animals are arthropods and there are more species of insects than all other animals put together. Here you will see why arthropods are such a diverse and successful group.

Arthropods are extremely adaptable animals. Different members of the group can feed on almost anything from blood to paper using specially adapted limbs and mouthparts.

Another factor contributing, in particular, to the success of insects is that young and adult animals may have completely different lifestyles. Caterpillars and adult butterflies, for example, have different diets and therefore do not compete with each other for food supplies. The immature form is transformed into an adult during a process called metamorphosis and the exhibit 'Changes' shows some fascinating film of this.

Many arthropods build nests but none are more spectacular than those of termites. A lifesize model of a termite mound with its underground nest and giant tower above is at the centre of the gallery. If you would like to see some live insects living in complex societies there a nest of fungus-growing ants in 'Insect societies'.

CRAWLIES'

Left: Fascinating
fungus-growing ants

Deadly stowaways

The presence of live spiders, and even scorpions, in consignments of
imported fruits, especially bananas and grapes, is becoming an increasing
problem. In the summer of 1988 thousands of pounds worth of
Californian grapes were destroyed by British supermarkets because of a
black-widow spider scare. Although the variety of imported tropical fruit
has increased, one important reason for the greater incidence of such
spiders is a reduction in the use of pesticides.

In order to assist with this problem, the Museum offers an identification
and advisory service to producers, wholesalers and retailers. This kind of
work is expected to lead to practical courses that will enable people from
the fruit trade to become familiar with some of the exotic species and to
recognize the dangerous ones.

To protect themselves, some
arthropods have evolved a fearsome
array of weapons. A scorpion, for
example, has claws, an armoured
body and a poisonous sting to
defend itself. Other arthropods have
more subtle methods - they use only
camouflage or coloured disguises for
protection.

Spiders and mites belong to an
arthropod group known as arachnids.
Although less familiar than spiders, mites
are more economically important. Some
mites help enrich the soil and kill pests
while others attack crops or cause
debilitating diseases.

Another group, the crustaceans, includes
lobsters, shrimps and crabs. In the sea,
crustaceans are a major source of food
for many fishes. Krill, the collective name
for small shrimp-like crustaceans, is the
sole source of food for baleen whales.
Just in case you imagine that your home
is free of arthropod intruders, pay a visit
to 1 Crawley House to see how closely
arthropods share all our lives.

Top: Investigate the
transformation of a
caterpillar
Centre: Peer into the
world of crustaceans
Bottom: A chance to see
a range of arthropod
colours

Right: This large model
scorpion is quite safe to
approach

Ladybirds & lobsters, scorpions & centipedes

DISCOVERY

Left: Making friends with the king of the jungle

The exhibition on the lower ground floor allows children to explore the natural world for themselves in exciting hands-on displays.

The Discovery Centre has been designed so that 7-11 year-old children can investigate each activity with their parents. Parents get involved helping their children make the most of the Centre.

Above: A conch shell. One of the many specimens you can examine on the 'Please touch' table
Circle: Art activities. Drawing a specimen

CENTRE

At the 'Please touch' table you can touch and talk about specimens such as a python skin or penguin's wing. Then test your wits with your fingertips to guess the 'Feely box' surprises. No peeking until you've made a thorough exploration!

Other activities give you the chance to experiment with processes that most people take for granted. In 'Flying seeds' you can cut out a seed shape and launch it into the breeze - but can you change the direction the 'seeds' spin in, or control how far they travel? And once you've worked out 'How fishes float', can you make the model fish float at the same level all the time? Expert staff are on hand to help you with your investigations.

During the Easter and summer holidays, the Discovery Centre hosts such special events as storytelling, model-making and art activities; Museum scientists give short talks about their work; and 'Focus point' trolleys trundle out to the four corners of the Museum.
On very busy days it may be necessary to restrict the numbers visiting the Centre at any one time. At these times tickets for half-hour sessions will be available from the Information Desk at the Museum entrance.

Opening hours
Monday - Friday 10.30 - 17.00
(during term-time, school groups have priority until 15.30)
Saturday 10.30 - 17.00
Sunday 11.30 - 17.00

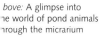
Above: A glimpse into the world of pond animals through the micrarium

Top: What can you feel in the 'Feely box'?
Centre: Launch a seed and watch it fly

Bottom: How sharp is the 'sword' of a swordfish? Find out on the 'Please touch' table

Below: Model of Charles Darwin and his study
Circle: 'A mutant in my garden!' Peter Collinson's peach tree suddenly produces a nectarine

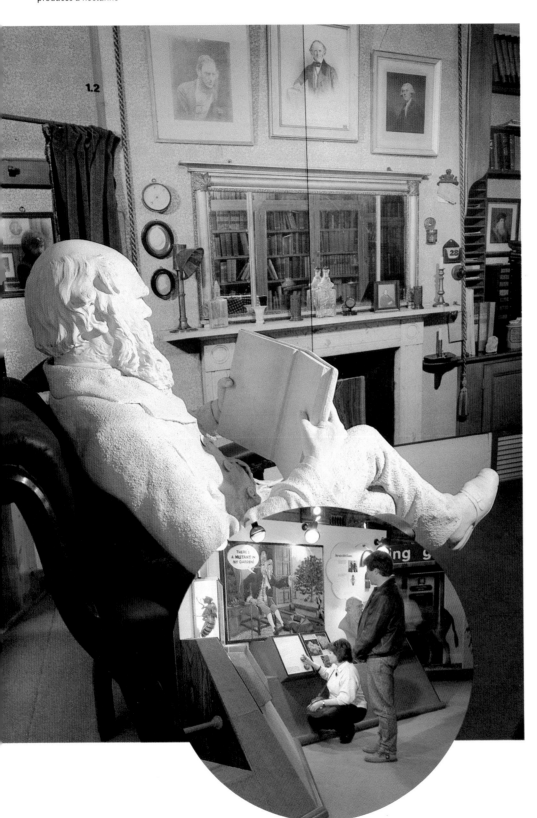

1.2

Have you ever wondered how there came to be so many different species on Earth? One explanation is that evolution, a process of gradual change over millions of years, has produced this enormous diversity.

Charles Darwin was one of th first people to propose a convincing theory which could account for changes within species that might eventually give rise to new species. In 1859 he published a book entitled *On the Origin of Species by Means of Natural Selection* and it is the process of natural selection that is explained in this exhibition.

Darwin had observed domestic or artificial selection at work in the breeding of plants and animals. By deliberately selecting certain characteristics in the individuals that are to be bred, people are able to produce changes in a wide variety of plant and animal species. In the exhibition, you can see how new kinds of dogs have been bred in this way.

SPECIES

Left: Breeders have produced different types of dogs by a process of selection over many generations
Centre: Survival of the fittest - who catches the worm?
Bottom: It was once thought that egg and sperm cells contained miniature replicas of the adults that produced them

Fussy about their food

Aphids (greenfly) are not only a nuisance on garden roses, they also pose a serious threat to agriculture. Large numbers of them devour our crops, often spreading plant virus diseases. Aphid pests come in many varieties - seven different species have been found on roses alone. By analysing the structure and arrangement of genes on their chromosomes, Museum scientists are helping to distinguish between the numerous species. Most aphids will only feed on a single species of plant, or on a few related kinds. Now Museum scientists are finding that aphids' eating habits are even more fastidious than we had suspected. Aphids colonizing sweet corn, for instance, were thought to come from related grasses growing as weeds in or near the cornfields; but although the weed-feeding aphids look the same as the sweet corn pests, they are genetically different. Thus weeds are not the source of the sweet corn aphids, and plans for controlling the pest can take this into account.

If an individual inherits a characteristic that makes it better adapted to its environment than other members of its species, it will have a better chance of survival. One example shown in the exhibition is that of a mouse with dark fur. Dark fur may provide better camouflage from predatory owls than light fur. The dark mouse will thus be more likely to survive to reproduce than its paler coloured relatives, and over several generations the proportion of dark mice in the whole population will increase.Because environments differ from place to place and may vary with time, over thousands of generations populations may adapt and change again and again. In some cases a population may become geographically divided and the separated groups change so much that they eventually become separate species.

Above: New genes can be brought into a population by migration and removed by selection
Below left: Discover what natural selection is and how it works

arwin developed his theory from everal other observations of species. e noticed that all living things can roduce far more offspring than are eeded to replace them, but not all the ffspring survive to reproduce. ving things must compete for limited esources, such as food and space. ometimes it is a matter of luck which urvive and which die. But because no vo members of a species are exactly ike, some may have an advantage ver others. This advantage may be ontrolled by the environment or by enes, which are passed on from one eneration to the next.

MAN'S PLACE

This exhibition considers the question of how human beings are related to other animals and the various 'fossil men' whose remains have been discovered in different parts of the world.

In order to consider these relationships, we must look closely at our own characteristics and then investigate whether or not they are shared by any other animals, living or extinct.

The evidence suggests that chimpanzees and gorillas are probably our closest living relatives because they share more of our characteristics than any other mammals. But neither of these animals walks upright and, for their size, they do not have such large brains as humans. So, we must look for closer relatives amongst the fossils. In the main part of the exhibition you can consider the evidence from different fossil groups. The australopithecines lived in Africa between 5 and 1.5 million years ago. From their skeletons we can tell that they were able to walk upright and were therefore more closely related to humans than chimpanzees and gorillas. Another group, the habilines, lived between 2 and 1.5 million years ago. They had larger brains than australopithecines and made a variety of tools. For this reason, habilines are thought to be even more closely related to us and are given the scientific name *Homo habilis* or 'handy man'.

Top: Contemplating the neandertals
Circle: Reconstruction of a neandertal burial based on remains found at Teshik-Tash, USSR

IN EVOLUTION

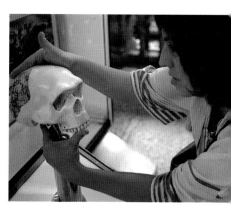

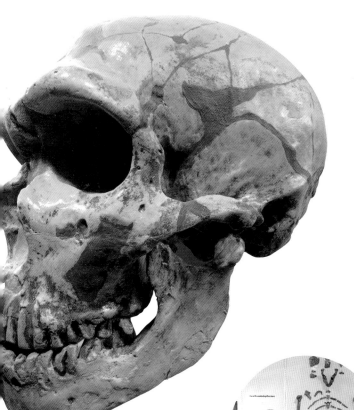

Top right: Inspired by our ancestors

Bottom: Feel the dent on the back of the neandertal skull

Left: Could this fossil ape be more closely related to us than other living apes?

nother unique human characteristic is
ur use of fire for heating and cooking.
Homo erectus people, whose remains
ave been found in the Far East, were
robably the first people to use fire.
hese people were taller than habilines
nd had larger brains so that they are
hought to be more closely related to us
han the habilines.
ut our closest known fossil relatives are
he neandertals, people who lived in
urope and the Middle East between
50 000 and 40 000 years ago. They
ad larger brains than *Homo erectus*
eople, they made tools, used fire and
uried their dead.
y about 100 000 years ago people like
s were living in Africa and the Middle
ast, and by 30 000 years were
habiting much of the world. Paintings
ade by these early people have been
ound in Africa, Asia, Europe and
ustralia and evidence suggests that they
ound food by hunting, but later began
 cultivate crops and keep animals.
heir early farming communities were
e beginnings of the towns and cities of
ur modern world.

'Lucy', the most famous
australopithecine, was
found in Ethiopia in 1974

Reconstruction of adult
female australopithecine

Neandertal woman
fashioning a spear

The origin of modern people

Despite differences in appearance, all people alive today are members of the species Homo sapiens*. What is less certain, however, is how modern humans originated. Some scientists think that we evolved from several different ancestors around the world and that gradually they intermixed and developed into modern humans. Others, including Museum scientists, believe that modern humans originated in one area only and then dispersed.*
Powerful support for the idea of a single origin for modern people has been obtained from studying fossils and genetics. The fossil record shows that modern-looking people were present in Africa 50 000 years before they appeared in Europe and the Far East, so Africa is thought to be the source of modern humans. This theory is supported by genetic evidence as modern African populations have a greater genetic diversity than European, Asian and Australasian populations. Since genetic diversity is a measure of the age of a population, this fact supports the theory that modern Homo sapiens *originated in Africa.*

Piltdown: a scientific forgery
by F Spencer

Man's place in evolution 2nd ed.

Below: Slice of the Mundrabilla iron meteorite found in Western Australia in 1966

Circle: Remarkable table top of ancient Roman marbles

MINERALS,

Rocks are composed of minerals which, like plants and animals, are an essential part of natural history - without them there would be no planet Earth and no life upon it.

Minerals and rocks have been represented in the British Museum's collections since its formation in 1753.

METEORIC IRON.

Above left: Sulphur from Sicily
Right: Bright blue opal in jasper

ear the entrance to the mineral gallery, here the science of mineralogy is troduced, there is a collection of ineral curios donated by the founder of e British Museum, Sir Hans Sloane. ese unusual bowls, rings and naments were transferred to South ensington in 1881.

e main part of the gallery is occupied cases of minerals displayed according their chemical composition and ucture. About 3000 different minerals e known and new ones are discovered ch year. They come in an amazing riety of colours and shapes.

emstones are minerals that are cut and ized for their beauty and durability. roughout the gallery there are some quisite examples of fine crystals and emstones. And, should you wish to see ore, there is another fine collection on splay in the *Gemstones* exhibition.

t the far end of the gallery is the pular meteorite pavilion. The Earth is ntinually bombarded with natural rock agments from space. Most burn up in e atmosphere, producing 'shooting ars', but if they reach the Earth's rface they are known as meteorites. together about 4000 different eteorites have been recovered and eces of about half of these are in the useum's collections.

The poor man's space probe

How did the Earth, sun and planets form? The study of meteorites is central to the attempts of scientists to answer this question. Most meteorites are fragments of asteroids (small planets) and have not been changed since the Earth was formed, 4550 million years ago. Some meteorites contain dust from stars which appeared near our sun at about the same time. By studying the chemical composition of meteorites, Museum scientists are beginning to understand the processes by which our sun, the Earth and other planets were formed. Because meteorites are samples of objects from space where few people have the chance to go, they have often been called 'the poor man's space probe'.

Above: Light brings gemstones to life

Minerals of Cornwall and Devon by P G Embrey & R F Symes

Meteorites: Key to our existence by Robert Hutchison & Andrew Graham

Gemstones by C M Woodward & R R Harding

The search for our Beginnings by R Hutchison

Minerals of the English Lake District, Caldbeck Fells by M Cooper & C Stanley

Rock Solid by Anna Grayson

Below: A family faces up to a pair of seals
Circle: Which of these fungi are good to eat and which are poisonous?

This exhibition was specifically designed for the amateur naturalist and countryside enthusiast.

NATURAL HISTORY

The gallery depicts a wide range of habitats, and features - as specimens, models or photographs - many of the animal and plant species found in Britain.

An introductory area traces changes in the British landscape, plants and animals from the last Ice Age, 20 000 years ago, to the present day. It then looks at the impact of human beings on the environment and suggests ways in which we can conserve natural habitats. Another exhibit introduces the principles of identification and gives you the chance to identify some real plants and animals.

The main exhibition, up the stairs, is divided into seven areas. These correspond to the major habitats recognized in Britain today: woodland; seashore; urban and wasteland; freshwater; field and downland; heath, moor and highland; and estuary, saltmarsh and sand dune. Each section shows some of the characteristic wildlife of that habitat as well as giving useful environmental information.

Top: Foxes are now a familiar sight in many cities
Bottom: The springtime courtship behaviour of brown hares gave rise to the saying ' ...as mad as a March hare'

A fishy tale

The River Thames has been an integral part of London's development as a city for nearly two thousand years. During this time the river has been put to a variety of uses, mainly to its detriment. The enormous increase in London's population in the 1800s sealed the river's fate. Untreated sewage and industrial waste were pumped directly into the river and soon large reaches of the Thames were almost devoid of fish. Although initial attempts to treat London's sewage resulted in some species of fish returning, a survey by a Museum scientist in 1957 revealed that there was no established fish population between Kew and Gravesend - a distance of over 60 kilometres.
Efforts made to clean up the Thames were again monitored by the Museum between 1967 and 1973. Around 100 species of fish were found living in the tidal reaches of the river. Today the Thames is probably cleaner than at any time in the last 400 years and is now home to about 130 species of fish, including salmon.

Bats: a natural history by J E Hill & J D Smith

Seals of the World 2nd ed. by J E King

Observing British and European Mammals by C Boulchardy & F Moutou

Finding and Identifying Mammals in Britain by G B Corbet

STORY OF THE

This exhibition tells the story of our planet from its formation in the stars, thousands of millions of years ago, to the present-day.

The entrance to the exhibition is through a dramatic rockface, cast from a road cutting in the Highlands of Scotland. The rock is metamorphic rock which formed one thousand million years ago, under the sea that originally covered northern Britain.

The story begins in outer space as the Earth was formed from elements in exploding stars. You can get some idea of Earth's place in the Universe by looking at the millions of other galaxies that surround us and then at our own. Within our galaxy is one star, our Sun, and orbiting around the Sun are the planets of our Solar System.

A little nearer is Earth's natural satellite, the Moon. In a separate exhibit you will find a sample of Moon rock which has been lent by NASA. Part of the rock is feldspar which is 4000 million years old - older than any rock known on Earth.

The Earth today is by no means unchanging. Large sections of its outer layers called 'plates' move small distances each year, eventually causing the formation of mountains and shaping of continents. The theory of 'plate tectonics', which explains these movements and their consequences, is explored in the exhibition.

The geology and fine details of the Earth's crust are affected by processes such as erosion, weathering and sedimentation. These are usually slow and undramatic. In contrast, volcanic eruptions can be sudden and devastating.

Above: Out of this world
Circle: The Crab Nebula, remains of a supernova blast

EARTH

Above: Weigh up the Earth's story for yourself
Below: Original moon rock

Left: Discover our planet's inner secrets

When a volcano erupts, magma - semi-molten rock from below the ground - is forced out from inside the Earth. Earthquakes, which can also produce dramatic changes, are caused by sudden movements or fractures of the Earth's crust that can occur at the edges of plates under pressure. You can experience how an earthquake feels in the exhibition's earthquake room.

A flight of steps near the earthquake room takes you up to *Time in the rocks*, a new set of displays about geological time. Here you will discover how the Earth gradually changes, and in a spectacular video you can watch the entire, 4000 million year history of the planet compressed into just a few minutes.

Far left: Telling rock-time is like looking through a pile of old newspapers

Left: The Earth's rocky past

The Story of the Earth by F W Dunning

Volcanoes by S van Rose & I F Mercer

Earthquakes by S van Rose

TREASURES OF THE

Treasures of the Earth examines the areas of geology which affect our lives - those concerned with the discovery, recovery and use of minerals and rocks.

The central feature of the exhibition is a house which demonstrates just how and where we use these substances obtained from the Earth.

Aggregates
Industrial sand
Building stone

Above: Minerals have many important uses
Circle: Discover the mineral treasures in your kitchen...or car (top right)

Limestone
Magnesia

Above: Pick a mineral and discover its secrets

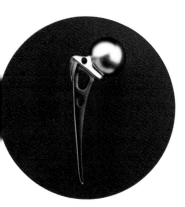

Left: We use minerals to make replacement hip joints containing vanadium, titanium and aluminium
Below: Wedgwood vase made from clay and sand with a cobalt pigment

Useful minerals

The Natural History Museum holds one of the great mineral collections of the world and its scientists are using samples from the collection to study how atoms are arranged in minerals. Each mineral has a distinct chemical composition of atoms which give it its characteristics - for example the hardness of diamond and the softness of talc. These differences mean that minerals can be used for a wide variety of purposes, including building materials, catalysts and electronic components.

In one Museum project, scientists are discovering how a small change in the atomic structure of a mineral can cause a dramatic change in the effect of a catalyst. (A catalyst is a chemical that encourages a reaction to happen.) In another, scientists are investigating how minerals in mine dumps react with the atmosphere. This work may help us understand how chemicals can seep from mine dumps into the water supply.

...ou can locate materials such as copper, ...ay, titanium and lead - all of which are ... be found in a typical kitchen, garage ... greenhouse.

...n animated film portrays the different ...eological environments in which useful ...inerals and rocks are found. Many ...inerals are found as ores which must ... dug up and purified and a large ...odel shows the workings of a large ...odern mine.

...lose by is a display of useful minerals, ...here you can inspect a collection of ...artly processed materials and domestic ...nd industrial objects, from artificial hip ...ints to railway lines. All of these ...ontain natural substances and any ...uestions you have about where such ...inerals are found, extracted and used, ...an be answered at one of the ...omputer-operated data banks.

Above: Superb specimens in a high-tech setting

GEMSTONES

Below: A large vase, made in 1868 from a form of fluorite called Blue John
Circle: The word 'opal' probably derives from the Sanskrit for 'precious stone'

Gemstones have been on display among the minerals at the Geological Museum since its earliest days.

When the new Geological Museum was laid out in 1935 the gems and decorative stones were taken out of the main mineral display and given pride of place in the centre of the ground floor where they can still be found today.

A gemstone is a mineral that has been cut or shaped for decoration. It will be beautiful, either by virtue of its colour, as in ruby, emerald or sapphire, or its sparkle, as in diamond. Although most gemstones are transparent, some have a silky sheen, such as moonstone, or a play of colours, such as opal. In many cultures gemstones are worn not only as objects of beauty, but as symbols of status and power. To serve this purpose they must be of the 'best' colour, flawless, large and rare.

Other decorative materials featured in the displays include carvings made from agate, jadeite and turquoise; rocks, such as serpentinite and lapis lazuli; and substances, such as amber, pearl, jet, ivory and coral, which were once a part of living creatures.

The gemstone display in the Museum aims to show the large number of minerals that can be used as gems. Here you can see the remarkable stones that can be cut from such little known minerals as kunzite, zoisite, andalusite and scapolite.

In every case cut and carved gemstones are displayed alongside natural crystals and, where appropriate, synthetic stones are displayed for comparison.

Above left and right: The Murchison Snuff Box, in daylight and ultraviolet light

Top left: A cut gemstone perched on a large spodumene crystal. *Centre:* Carved jade on a carved ivory stand. *Bottom:* Carved lapis lazuli bowl mounted on ormolu

Agates by H McPherson

Gemstones by C M Woodward & R R Harding

Crystals by I F Mercer

BRITAIN BEFORE MAN

The continents act as the history books of the Earth - they carry a record of events and environments that stretches back to the origin of the Earth itself.

Britain before Man investigates the record preserved in one small patch of the Earth's crust, the north-western edge of the Eurasian continental mass.

The exhibition shows the history of Britain long before the appearance of its people or the coastline that we know today.

The story that emerges is one of four long, relatively tranquil geological eras when layers of rock were laid down under the sea or on land to produce fou 'structural storeys' in Britain. Separating these times were shorter, more turbulent episodes during which the layers were bent and broken, volcanoes were active and mountains were formed.

In the exhibition, Britain's story is told with a series of dioramas, paintings and models that reconstruct the ancient land and its animals and plants. You will also find many specimens of the rocks that have shaped the British Isles, as well as photographs of present-day landscapes.

Below: Trafalgar Square, London, 100 000 years ago

Right: Around 670 million years ago a great ice sheet moved over an area that is now Scotland
Far right: Life on the floor of the chalk sea

Britain Before Man by F W Dunning

Left: Rapid evolution of these fossil ammonites has provided geologists with a valuable time key

BRITISH FOSSILS

Left: Bony fish from Rochester, Kent

ove: View of the gallery showing the 'fossil wall'

The remains or traces of long dead animals and plants preserved in rock are known as fossils.

In Britain, fossils can be found in the rocks of all the main geological periods.

They can be used to trace ancient environments in the study of evolution, or as evidence to date rocks.

The exhibition of *British fossils* attempts to answer the following questions: where are fossils found? how do we give them names? what exactly are they? Large models show some well-known fossil animals, such as trilobites and ammonites, and the fossil trees that formed our coal.

Fossils can be collected by anyone who knows where to look for them. A video programme will give you hints on how to start up as a fossil collector.

A large part of the exhibition is devoted to a collection of British fossils that you can use for reference. They are displayed in a series of cases according to their geological age - all the fossils from any one rock formation are arranged together. Each section gives information about the geography and climate of the time periods and the localities in which particular rock formations can be seen.

A fossil's fate

Fossils arrive at the Museum from three sources - the Museum's staff, amateur collectors and professional fossil hunters. In the palaeontology laboratories, fossils are extracted from the surrounding rock and cleaned to allow identification. Some fossil types can be recognized immediately, but if the fossil is from a poorly known locality or of an entirely unknown species, identification can be very complicated.

Once identified, the fossil can be used to investigate how the ancient creature lived. Such research may help to elucidate the reasons why some species have survived over millions of years, while others have become extinct.

Top left: Ammonite marble from Marston Magna, Somerset
Bottom: Bed of crinoids from Lyme Regis, Dorset

British Fossils Identification (3 book set)

Owls, Caves and Fossils by P J Andrews

Fossils: The key to the past by R A Fortey

BRITAIN'S OFFSHORE

Below: Both decks are crammed with exhibits
Left circle: Advanced video techniques bring the North Sea to life
Right circle: Production platform models, accurate to the last detail

This modern exhibition is sponsored by U.K.O.O.A. (United Kingdom Offshore Operators Association), an organization that represents the oil and gas companies operating in British waters.

In keeping with its subject matter, the exhibition is designed in the form of an oil platform with two decks.

The lower deck features the geology of the Earth's crust under the sea around Britain. Here you can discover how the forces caused by gradual movements of continents have formed and shaped oil-bearing rocks, and how the lush, swampy rain forest that covered these areas 300 million years ago now provides Britain's oil and gas reserves.

OIL & GAS

Top: Hunting for North Sea treasure with a seismic map
Bottom: Make your own 'decision to drill'

Left: Climb on board the production platform

e formation of these reserves is, to a ge extent, a matter of chance, quiring not only the correct mbination of rock type and structure, t also a specific sequence of vironmental changes.

hibits on the upper deck explain the phisticated exploration technology ed to locate oil and gas. A promising sult from a preliminary seismic survey ads to test drillings, rock sampling and mputer modelling of the land beneath e sea. All of these are needed in order assess whether or not the vast costs constructing a production platform n be justified.

The size and type of oil platform which is built to extract oil and gas depends on many factors including the depth of the sea and the distance of the 'find' from land. Large-scale models of several different oil platforms show how oil and gas are obtained and transferred to land for our use.

A separate section of the exhibition outlines the history of the exploration of our offshore waters from the first discovery of gas in 1965 and of oil in 1970. It explains the many issues, such as international boundaries, licensing and safety factors that have been considered over the years.

There are several videos in the exhibition. 'Liquid assets', at the centre of the exhibits, tells the story of the formation, discovery and development of offshore oil (best viewed from upstairs). In the video theatre, a series of programmes shows how oil platforms are built and operated. There's also an instructive cartoon for younger visitors.

MINERAL

Left: Slate from Welsh quarries, such as the Penrhyn Quarry, is used for roofing all over Britain

The second floor of the Museum's Earth Galleries was laid out in 1935 as a showcase of rocks and minerals of economic importance.

Since then the maps and diagrams have been updated, but on the whole the gallery retains its pre-war appearance.

One side of the floor is taken up by metals such as iron, lead, zinc and copper. The other has displays of the precious metals, gold and silver, together with the non-metallic material such as sulphur, graphite, phosphates and abrasives.

Overall, the gallery shows the geology of the minerals and rocks that were most important in 1935. Many features such as the copper mines of Cornwall and silver mines of Freiberg, are now of special historic interest.

The many rock specimens on display help build up a picture of the typical geology of each ore. For example, platinum is exhibited with the dark igneous rock in which it is found. Many other cases contain beautiful examples of the ore minerals and the minerals which are found with them, known as the 'gangue'. The lead-zinc exhibit, for instance, contains many lovely specimens of galena, sphalerite, calcite fluorite and dolomite.

The displays are full of amusing and interesting curiosities. Look out for the delicate graphite carvings and the case of rock salt which includes a necklace that you would be ill-advised to wear out of doors in Britain!

Above: Early Victorian panel made entirely of stone from Britain and Ireland
Left: Baryte from Cumbria

DEPOSITS
OF THE WORLD

*nerals from the
llection of Henry
dlam, a Piccadilly
sier, who bequeathed
000 minerals to the
useum in 1880
p:* Torbernite from
rnwall
iddle: Pyromorphite
m Cornwall
ove: Calcite from
umbria

Cornish gold

*Records of gold in Cornwall date from the sixteenth century. In river
valleys and streams, gold is often associated with resistant minerals such
as cassiterite, and usually occurs as plates or small nuggets. The largest
nugget, weighing nearly 60 grams, was found in 1808 in the Carnon
Stream Tin Works, near Truro.*

*Although there is little recoverable gold in the tin, copper, lead and zinc
deposits of the area, gold has been found in some of the antimony mines
of north Cornwall. By studying the minerals associated with the gold,
Museum scientists are trying to discover its origin. They may also be able
to predict other likely sources of this most precious of metals.*

This diorama of a
Northampton ironstone
quarry in 1935 is of
historic interest because
ironstone is no longer
mined in Britain

Minerals of Cornwall and Devon
by P G Embrey & R F Symes

Minerals of the English Lake District: Caldbeck Fells
by M P Cooper & C Stanley

ORIGINS OF THE

Circle: Earth Galleries entrance of The Natural History Museum, formerly the Geological Museum

The Natural History Museum in South Kensington began as a department of the British Museum in Bloomsbury.

The immense private collection of Sir Hans Sloane, a wealthy physician, formed the basis of the British Museum.

On his death, in 1753, he bequeathed his collection to the nation, in return for a payment of £20 000 to his heirs. The money was raised by private lottery and the British Museum was founded the same year.

At first his countless animal, plant and mineral specimens, coins, manuscripts and other treasures were kept together in Bloomsbury. But, over the years, as new objects poured in, shortage of space became a major problem. In 1860, a momentous decision was taken to move the natural history collection from Bloomsbury to a new location. Part of the site of the 1862 International Exhibition in South Kensington was acquired for the new museum, and the architect Alfred Waterhouse was commissioned to design a suitable building. He was to follow guidelines set out by Dr Richard Owen, a distinguished anatomist, who was Superintendent of the Natural History Departments at the British Museum.

In 1881, after seven years of construction beset with difficulties, the Museum first opened its doors to an enthusiastic public.

The Natural History Museum remained, administratively, a part of the British Museum until 1963 when it became an independent institution.

MUSEUM

Top: Montagu House in Bloomsbury - the first home of the British Museum
Bottom: Cartoon from Comic News in 1863, showing the removal of animal specimens from Bloomsbury to South Kensington

Left: Staircase near the entrance of the old British Museum, Montagu House, in 1845

...nce then there has been another great ...ange. In 1985, The Natural History ...useum took over the care of its ...ighbour, the Geological Museum, ...om the British Geological Survey. ...unded in 1835, the Geological ...useum was an offshoot of the ...eological Survey. Henry De la Beche, ...under of the Survey, was employed by ...e Government to investigate the ...ology of Devon. In 1835 he pointed ...t to the Chancellor of the Exchequer ...at, as he would inevitably amass ...cks, minerals and fossils during his

work, it would be both useful and inexpensive for the Government to set up a museum. Rooms were provided in Craig's Court, off Whitehall, and the Museum came into being.
The tiny galleries were soon full and so, in 1851, the collections were moved to a new building, near Piccadilly, opened as The Museum of Practical Geology. But by the 1920s this building had to be condemned and the rebirth of the Museum came in 1935 at a new site in South Kensington.

To consolidate the recent merger of The Natural History and Geological Museums, *Lasting Impressions*, a spacious, modern gallery connecting the two buildings, was opened in 1988. The expanded Natural History Museum now offers visitors the opportunity to explore the Earth and its life, both past and present, under one roof.

...ght: Sir Hans Sloane, the ...under of the British ...useum. Sloane Square ...d Hans Crescent were ...med in his honour
...ntre: Henry De la ...che (1796-1855), the ...under of the Geological ...useum
...r right: Richard Owen, a ...lled anatomist, was the ...st person to coin the ...rd 'dinosaur' (Greek ...'terrible lizard')

Sir Hans Sloane's collection, which formed the basis of the Museum, was probably the largest assembled by any private individual in eighteenth-century Europe.

Apart from some 50 000 books there were over 10 000 animal specimens, 334 volumes of pressed plants and a large number of minerals, rocks and fossils.

Although most of the animal specimens have perished, all 334 volumes of his herbarium have survived and even today are an important source of biological information.

During the first 40 years of the British Museum's existence the collections grew mainly as a result of British interest overseas. The most notable voyages of discovery were probably those of Captain Cook. In 1768, on his first voyage around the world, he was accompanied by a wealthy naturalist called Joseph Banks, who donated a considerable amount of material to the Museum.

Banks selected skilled natural history illustrators and artists to accompany him on this voyage. One of them, Sydney Parkinson, completed three volumes of animal drawings and eighteen of beautifully depicted plants, which remai part of the Museum's extensive collection of original drawings. (Today, The Natural History Museum holds the third largest collection of watercolour drawings, after the British Museum and the Victoria and Albert Museum).

Above: Sir Joseph Banks (1743 - 1820). This statue used to stand in Montagu House, the first home of the British Museum; it can now be found on the second floor
Circle: Part of a unique collection of 65 mounted cassowaries, bequeathed to the Museum by Lord Rothschild on his death in1937

COLLECTION

Above: A specimen of *Banksia* collected on Cook's first voyage and named in honour of Joseph Banks

Top: Coral specimens collected during the *Beagle* voyage with Darwin's original label
Above: Weedy sea dragons drawn by Ferdinand Bauer on Matthew Flinders' circumnavigation of Australia in HMS *Investigator* between 1802 and 1803

the ninteenth century the number of specimens in the collections increased prodigiously through expeditions made specifically for scientific reasons. Among the early acquisitions were specimens from Darwin's voyage on HMS *Beagle*, the entire museum of the Zoological Society of London and of the East India Company.

The growth of the collections now amounts to around half a million additions each year. Increasingly, collecting is more specific and is carried out by Museum scientists who tend to concentrate not only on gathering species, but also on observing them in their natural habitats.

Right: Platypus by Ferdinand Bauer

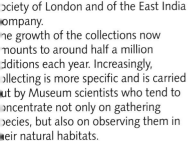

❀ **Sir Joseph Banks** by H B Carter

❀ **The Chelsea Gardener: Philip Miller 1691 - 1771** by H Le Rougetel

❀ **Art in Natural History Vol I: Ferdinand Bauer** by Marlene Norst

Below: Removing the surrounding stone from a fossil using dental drills

Unseen by most visitors to The Natural History Museum is the vast collection of more than 65 million specimens and one million books and manuscripts, which comprise the most complete collection of natural history material in the world.

To care for and organize the wealth of information contained within it, there are more than 300 scientists and librarians working behind the scenes.

Circle: Skeletons abound in the osteology storeroom

SCENES

Above: Behind the Museum's facade a jumble of rooftops conceals its treasures
Far left: Modern electron microscopes can magnify objects as much as a million times
Centre: The General Herbarium contains nearly two million specimens of flowering plants and conifers
Left: In the Spirit Building there are 4.5 kilometres of shelves devoted to fishes alone

The research conducted by Museum staff on particular groups of animals, plants, minerals or fossils is internationally renowned. It is used to resolve a diverse range of problems worldwide, often involving doctors, farmers, conservationists, and specialists in the fishing and oil industries. Some of these applied research projects are mentioned in the exhibition sections of this guide.

EXHIBITIONS

Below: The fishes gallery in 1911 (just after installation of the first electric lights).

When The Natural History Museum first opened at South Kensington on 18 April 1881, the displays made little attempt to go beyond a brief description of what the specimens were and where they came from.

Visitors were expected to educate themselves and, as one scientist wrote at the time, if they left with '... nothing but sore feet, a bad headache and a general idea that the animal kingdom is a mighty maze ...' then it was not considered to be the fault of the displays.

Circle: Will it work? Evaluation of an exhibit

& PUBLIC SERVICES

The first galleries echoed the Victorians' tastes and ideas, and were limited by the display techniques that were available. However, over the last hundred years, the public galleries have changed dramatically.

In 1972, a programme of exhibition renewal was begun that is still underway. Using advanced and innovative methods of display to interest and entertain visitors of all ages, new-style exhibitions put natural history in context. They aim to show not only the diversity of the natural world, but also some of the underlying principles of science - such as how natural forms have evolved and how living things interact with each other and with their non-living surroundings.

The first of these exhibitions, *Human biology*, was completed in 1977 and in 1980, largely as a result, the Museum was awarded the coveted title of 'Museum of the Year'. Since then many other permanent exhibitions have been developed.

The Museum's visitors vary tremendously in age, interest and in the time they have available to spend in the galleries. For enhancing or interpreting exhibitions there are books and leaflets and special public events. For more information about Museum services for adults and children, please refer to pages 50 and 51.

DESIGN

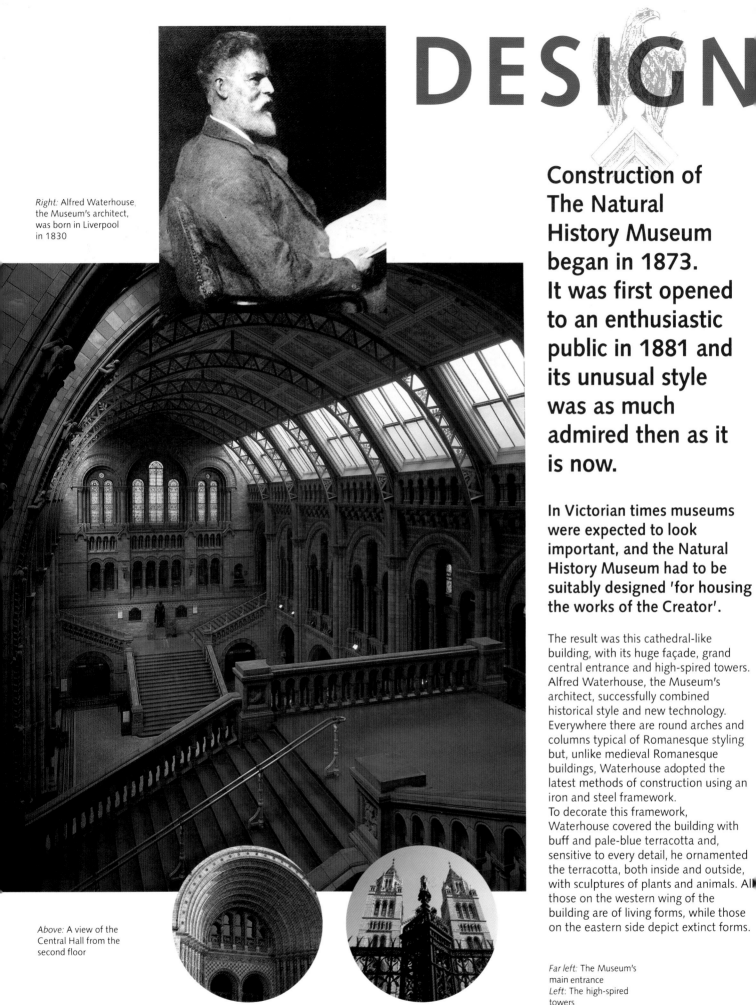

Right: Alfred Waterhouse, the Museum's architect, was born in Liverpool in 1830

Construction of The Natural History Museum began in 1873. It was first opened to an enthusiastic public in 1881 and its unusual style was as much admired then as it is now.

In Victorian times museums were expected to look important, and the Natural History Museum had to be suitably designed 'for housing the works of the Creator'.

The result was this cathedral-like building, with its huge façade, grand central entrance and high-spired towers. Alfred Waterhouse, the Museum's architect, successfully combined historical style and new technology. Everywhere there are round arches and columns typical of Romanesque styling but, unlike medieval Romanesque buildings, Waterhouse adopted the latest methods of construction using an iron and steel framework.
To decorate this framework, Waterhouse covered the building with buff and pale-blue terracotta and, sensitive to every detail, he ornamented the terracotta, both inside and outside, with sculptures of plants and animals. All those on the western wing of the building are of living forms, while those on the eastern side depict extinct forms.

Above: A view of the Central Hall from the second floor

Far left: The Museum's main entrance
Left: The high-spired towers

Above: Waterhouse's architecture deserves as much attention as the displays

Left: Waterhouse's pencil sketch of a grey heron for a terracotta pannel

hrough the huge Cromwell Road ntrance, visitors enter the great Central all, which is like the nave of a athedral. At the end of the Hall a single rand staircase divides at a landing and imbs up to the first floor galleries. acing back towards the entrance there a fine view of the arched bridge aircase that leads to the second floor nd from this bridge a bird's eye view own into the Central Hall.

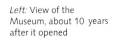

Left: View of the Museum, about 10 years after it opened

Alfred Waterhouse and The Natural History Museum
by M Girouard

Below: The Museum as it looks today
Circle: The upper balcony

The origin of the Zoological Museum is the result of one man's obsession for collecting. That man was Lionel Walter Rothschild.

At the age of 21 he was given a piece of land in Tring Park, Hertfordshire, by his father, the first Baron Rothschild and there he built two cottages - one to house his vast collection of insects and books and the other to house a caretaker.

A much larger building was also constructed to display Rothschild's mounted specimens. This was the beginning of the Zoological Museum. The Museum first opened to the public in August 1892 but by then Walter Rothschild had entered the family banking business so two professional curators were put in charge of the Museum. One of their first duties was to put the collections into order. Already there were over 4000 mammal and bird specimens on display while the study collections included more than 40 000 bird skins and over 500 000 insects. To cope with these vast numbers and provide more space for the library and public galleries, extensions to the Museum were constructed between 1908 and 1912.

Although under no obligation to display his collections, Rothschild was devoted to the public galleries.

MUSEUM, TRING

He would personally select the finest
specimens and then invite the best
taxidermists to prepare them. The
resulting displays were, for their time,
the finest to be seen anywhere.
Among the many unusual specimens
currently on display are a collection of
domestic dogs, an extremely rare
specimen of the quagga (one of only 16
in the world) and the Museum's famous
dressed fleas.
Walter Rothschild died in 1937,
bequeathing his entire collections to the
Trustees of the British Museum.

Below: A lifesize
reconstruction of the
extinct giant moa - the
largest bird that ever
lived

Above: Young visitors
standing in awe of the
mighty gorilla
Right: The giant moa
illustrated in Rothschild's
1907 book *Extinct birds*

Information Desk

Once inside the Museum be sure to visit the Information Desk, in front of the dinosaur *Diplodocus*. Staff here will be happy to inform you about the exhibitions and any special events occuring on that day. If you are bringing children, the Information Desk has a wide range of activity sheets for children of all ages to use in the galleries.

Public Events

The Museum organizes a diverse range of events for visitors of all ages. In your free leaflet you will find news of theatrical events, films, children's workshops, lectures, competitions, guided tours and new exhibitions. Admission to all events is free.

Museum Shops

The book and gift shops offer a wide range of natural history and geology books, maps, model dinosaurs, mineral specimens, sketch books, colouring books and many souvenir items, including jewellery and ceramics.

Refreshments

The Museum Restaurant offers a large range of hot and cold food, from home-made soup and salad platters to hot pies, baked potatoes and vegetables.
Under the Central Hall arches, the Waterhouse Café offers a range of café-style refreshments. For self-caterers, there's the Snack Bar, available to families during the school holidays and at weekends, next to the Activity Centre picnic area where you can buy a little something to go with your packed lunch. There is also a picnic area on the 1st floor of the Earth Galleries.

Facilities for the Disabled

Wheelchairs are available at the main and side entrances of the Museum. For assistance please contact any guide.

A wide range of products is featured in the mail order catalogue

Shopping by Post

Many Museum products and an unusual selection of toys and gifts may be ordered by post. Please write to the Museum's Marketing department for a free illustrated mail order catalogue.

Hire of the Museum

The Natural History Museum is a spectacular and prestigious venue for social and business entertaining of all kinds. For information about facilities and charges please contact the Functions Manager (071-938 8934).

The Central Hall provides a memorable venue for parties

Visitor Resources

The Museum's exhibitions and building provide an excellent stimulus and educational resource for the study of earth and life sciences. To meet the specialist needs of our visitors - both adults and children of all ages - the Museum offers wide-ranging services including tours for young children, activity sheets that interpret the exhibitions for children and young adults, and field trips.
For current details, visit the Information Desk in the Central Hall.

Face-painting is just one of many public events

Discovery Centre

Designed with 7-11 year old children and their parents in mind, the Discovery Centre offers opportunities to examine aspects of nature at close quarters.
Open Monday-Friday 10.30–17.00 (during term time school groups have priority until 15.30) Saturday 10.30–17.00 Sunday 11.30–17.00.
For those who can't get to London, a travelling version of the Discovery Centre journeys throughout the United Kingdom. To find out more telephone 071-938 9376

Teachers' Centre

This reference centre offers teachers the opportunity to gather information and ideas for teaching natural history whether in the Museum, the classroom, or outdoor Here you can find out about the services that the Museum offers for schools, collec samples of activity sheets and browse through a collection of useful books, posters and visual aids. The Centre is open 11.30–14.00 each weekday and the first Sunday of each month 14.00–17.00.

SERVICES

Teachers Courses

The Museum offers a variety of general and specific topic courses for teachers and student teachers. For details of the topics covered please write to Visitor Resources Section.

The Development Trust

The Natural History Museum Development Trust has been established to stimulate financial support for a wide range of Museum programmes. Under the patronage of HRH The Princess of Wales, the Trust aims to raise funds from sponsors and donors for important scientific research, exhibitions and education. For more information contact the Director, The Natural History Museum Development Trust, at the Museum's address, or telephone 071-938 8926/8786.

Membership Programme

Enquiries about the Museum's Membership Programme should be addressed to Jane Bevan at the Museum, telephone 071-938 9089.

The Scientist Corner in the Discovery Centre

The Rare Book Room, part of the General Library, houses many original natural history drawings and paintings as well as books and manuscripts

Recorded Information and General Enquiries

For 24-hour information on films, talks and exhibitions ring 042-692 7654. For other enquiries call 071-938 9123.

Library Services

With more than 800 000 volumes and 20 000 periodical titles covering all aspects of natural history, the Museum is well placed to serve the needs of the most demanding researchers.
Intending users should make an appointment prior to their visit, by calling 071-938 9191.
Library services include an online information retrieval service, which provides for scanning and listing of abstracts from several major databases,tailored to researchers' requests.Charges for this and other facilities will be given on request.

THE NATURAL HISTORY MUSEUM

Cromwell Road
London SW7 5BD
Telephone: 071-938 9123

Opening times:
Monday to Saturday 10.00 - 17.50
Sunday 11.00 - 17.50

Closed 23 - 26 December,
1 January

INDEX